THE NEW CHURCH ANTHEM BOOK

THE
NEW CHURCH
ANTHEM
BOOK

ONE HUNDRED ANTHEMS

Compiled and Edited by

LIONEL DAKERS

Music Department
OXFORD UNIVERSITY PRESS
Oxford and New York

Oxford University Press, Walton Street, Oxford OX2 6DP, England
Oxford University Press, 200 Madison Avenue, New York, NY 10016, USA

Oxford is a trade mark of Oxford University Press

1 3 5 7 9 10 8 6 4 2

Printed and bound in Portugal
on acid-free paper
by Printer Portuguesa

PREFACE

When *The Church Anthem Book* first appeared in 1933 it was obviously very much a child of its time which, I imagine, is how *The New Church Anthem Book* may well be viewed in sixty or more years' time. Even so, the aims of this new collection, and the policy underlining the choice of its contents, are in no way different from the first edition which proudly proclaimed, 'The aim of this book has been to choose and assemble one hundred approved anthems old and new...'

The role of the anthem, and its place not only in parish church worship but within Christian worship generally, is as assured and as relevant today as ever. The purpose of the *The New Church Anthem Book* is to encourage the use of a wide range of reasonably simple and singable music. Where, in the old edition, organ accompaniments were unnecessarily thick, and consequently awkward to negotiate, these have been thinned out, and in a number of instances note values have been halved and bar lengths altered in the interests of musical and visual clarity. The needs of depleted or incomplete choirs, which today are very much a reality, have also been taken into account.

We have taken advantage of the wide range of scholarship which was not so readily available sixty years ago. As a result, the music of each period has been edited by an accredited scholar. What I believe we have achieved, therefore, is as accurate as possible in terms of up to the minute scholarship.

Although tastes may change, over the years they generally widen. A comparison between this book and its predecessor will reveal that about one third of the original contents have been discarded. These include most of the excerpts from oratorios, together with other examples which today seem strangely ill-assorted or irrelevant. In their place come a number of reasonably simple pieces by contemporary composers whose names have in recent years become well known and whose works are respected with good reason in church music circles.

Where no editor's name is shown against a particular piece, I am responsible for any markings shown in square brackets. These, and any other similar guidelines, all of which are intended to be as simple as possible, are consistent with current editorial practice. English singing translations have been added in many cases, but it is hoped that choirs will use the original language whenever possible. The spelling and punctuation of Tudor English texts has normally been made consistent and modernized; where, however, a twentieth-century composer has set older words with original spelling, that has been retained. There is every reason to believe that, in the late sixteenth century, organs were used to support some or all of the voice parts; performers today should therefore feel free to accompany such 'unaccompanied' anthems when appropriate.

As with any composite collection of church music spanning the centuries, a general editor cannot possibly hope to please everyone. There are bound to be inclusions and omissions which may cause some surprise, but nevertheless I believe this to be a representative collection in which the realistic needs of most average situations have been borne in mind. That is certainly my intention.

LIONEL DAKERS

CONTENTS

SELECT LITURGICAL INDEX

Anthems which do not require full SATB choirs:

Anthems with parts which may be sung by congregations:

Commissioned by the Chancel Choir, First United Methodist Church, Omaha, USA, for Mel Olson

1. A Gaelic Blessing

Words adapted from
an old Gaelic rune

John Rutter
(b. 1945)

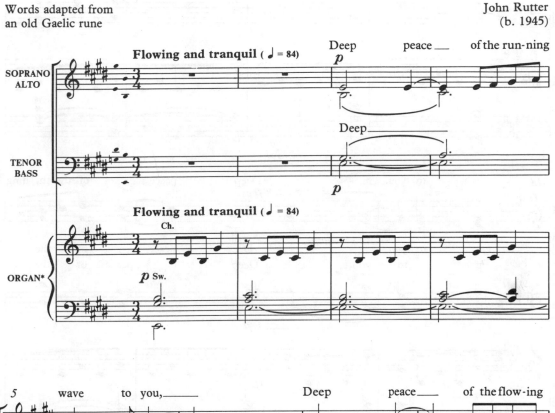

*The right hand of the organ part may alternatively be played on guitar.

2. A Palm Sunday Antiphon

Matthew 21: 9

David C. Morgan
(b. 1946)

-san - na to the Son of Da - vid.

-san - na to the Son of Da - vid.

dim.

Meno mosso

mp

Bless - ed,   bless - ed be the

mp

Bless - ed,   bless - ed be the

Meno mosso

mf   dim.   *p*

Ped.

King,   Bless - ed be the King__ that com - eth,   that

King,   Bless - ed be the King__ that com - eth,   that

com - eth in the name of the Lord, in the name of ___ the

com - eth in the name of the Lord, in the name of ___ the

Tempo primo

Lord.   Ho -

Lord.   Ho -

Tempo primo

-san - na,   Ho - san - na,   Ho - san - na to the

-san - na,   Ho - san - na,   Ho - san - na to the

Man.

3. Above all praise

Op. 79 No. 3

Felix Mendelssohn
(1809–47)

Shortened version, adapted for SATB chorus

4. Adoramus te, Christe

Antiphon, Feast of the Holy Cross

Giovanni Pierluigi da Palestrina
(c. 1526–94)

All dynamics are editorial.

5. Almighty and everlasting God

Orlando Gibbons
(1583–1625)
edited by
Peter le Huray
and David Willcocks

Collect for the Third
Sunday after Epiphany

All dynamics are editorial.

6. Almighty God, which hast me brought

Thomas Ford
(c. 1580–1648)
edited by
Nicholas Steinitz

William Leighton
(fl. 1603–1614)

All dynamics are editorial.

7. Antiphon

George Herbert
(1593–1633)

Philip Moore
(b. 1943)

The original version of this Antiphon for eight part choir is published by the RSCM.

No_ door ____ can   keep __ them   out;

No_ door ____ can   keep __ them   out;

No_ door ____ can   keep __ them   out;

No_ door ____ can   keep __ them   out;

ALTO

But a-bove all,

8. Ave verum corpus

Fourteenth-century hymn, sometimes attributed
to Pope Innocent VI (d. 1342)

William Byrd
(1543–1623)
edited by
John Morehen

This anthem may be sung a semitone higher.

All dynamics are editorial.

9. Ave verum corpus

Op. 2 No. 1

Fourteenth-century hymn, sometimes attributed
to Pope Innocent VI (d. 1342)

Edward Elgar
(1857–1934)

10. Ave verum corpus
K618

Fourteenth-century hymn, sometimes attributed
to Pope Innocent VI (d. 1342)

W. A. Mozart
(1756–91)

All dynamics are editorial.

11. Awake, thou wintry earth

From Cantata 129
Gelobet sei der Herr, mein Gott
(Trinity Sunday)

J. S. Bach (1685–1750)
Transcribed for organ by
Richard Marlow

A - wake thou win - try earth,   Fling
De - scend - ed to the grave,   Where

For Gerald Knight, and composed for the Official Opening of the new Headquarters
of The Royal School of Church Music at Addington Palace, Croydon
10 July, 1954

12. Behold, the tabernacle of God

Sarum Antiphon for the
Dedication of a Church

William H. Harris
(1883–1973)

13. Blest are the pure in heart

John Keble
(1792–1866)

H. Walford Davies
(1869–1941)

14. Blessed be the God and Father

Samuel Sebastian Wesley
(1810–1876)
edited by Lionel Dakers

I Peter

faith un - to sal - va - tion rea-dy to be re - veal-ed in the last

SOPRANO (SOLO)

time. But as

He which hath call - ed you is ho - ly, so be ye

Sw. Reed

Man.

ho - ly in all man-ner of ___ con - ver - sa - tion. Pass the

107 TENOR and BASS
f
Be - ing born a - gain, not of cor-rup-ti - ble seed, but of in - cor-

108
- rup - ti - ble, by the word of God. For all flesh is as grass, and all the

112
glo - ry of man as the flow - er of grass. The grass with-er-eth, and the

115
flow-er____ there-of fall — eth a - way:

Sw. Reed

Ped.

ff

15. Blessed is he that considereth

Psalm 41

Michael Wise
(1648–1687)
edited by
Christopher Dearnley

All dynamics are editorial, except where indicated.

*This dynamic is original.

58

up, raise — thou me up, and I shall re - ward_____ them.

— thou me up, raise thou me up, and I_____ shall re-ward them.

— thou me up, raise thou me up, and I shall re - ward, re - ward them.

62 SOPRANO
FULL *mf*

Bless - ed be the Lord God of Is - ra - el, Bless - ed be the Lord God of

ALTO
FULL *mf*

Bless - ed be the Lord God of Is - ra - el, Bless - ed be the Lord God of

TENOR
FULL *mf*

Bless - ed be the Lord God of Is - ra - el, Bless - ed be the Lord God of

BASS
FULL *mf*

Bless - ed be the Lord God of Is - ra - el, Bless - ed be the Lord God of

mf

16. Call to remembrance

Richard Farrant
(d. 1581)
edited by
Anthony Greening

Psalm 25: 5-6

All dynamics are editorial.

17. Cantate Domino

Psalm 148
translated by
Francis Jackson
(b. 1917)

Giuseppe Ottavio Pitoni
(1657–1743)
edited by R. R. Terry

18. Come down, O Love divine

Bianco da Siena
Tr. by R. F. Littledale

William H. Harris
(1883–1973)

Come down, O Love di-vine, Seek thou this soul of mine, And

vis - it it with thine own ar-dour glow - ing; O Com-fort - er draw

near,   With - in my heart ap – pear, And kin - dle it, thy

ho – ly flame be - stow - ing. _____

O let it free – ly burn,   Till earth-ly pas - sions turn   To

Man.

19. Come, Holy Ghost

Thomas Attwood
(1765–1838)
edited by Lionel Dakers

tr. John Cosin
(1594–1672)

Come, Ho - ly__ Ghost, our souls in - spire, And light - en

with ce - les - tial fire. Thou the a - noint - ing Spi - rit

art, Who dost thy sev - en - fold gifts im - part.__ Thy bless - ed

104

20. Come, ye faithful

St. John Damascene
tr. J. M. Neale

R. S. Thatcher
(1888–1957)

77

_f_

Al – – – le - lu – –

TENOR and BASS (and CONGREGATION ad lib.)

_ff_

Nei – ther might the gates___ of death, Nor   the tomb's dark por –

84

– ia!   Al – – le –

– tal,   Nor   the watch – ers, nor___ the seal, Hold   thee   as   a

91

– lu – – ia!

mor – – tal;   But___ to - day   a – midst___ the twelve

21. Comfort, O Lord, the soul of thy servant

from the Anthem *Be merciful unto me*

Psalm 86 v. 4

William Crotch
(1775–1847)

22. Crux fidelis

Venantius Fortunatus (530–609)
Translated by J. M. Neale

John IV, King of Portugal
(d. 1656)

for rehearsal only

All dynamics are editorial.

23. Drop, drop, slow tears

Phineas Fletcher
(1582–1650)

Orlando Gibbons
(1583–1625)
arranged by D. F. R. Wilson

All dynamics are editorial.

"This little piece is not exceeded by any foreign work of the kind. It should have been an Anthem, as it deserves a better fate than occasional performance by a Madrigal Society." S. S. Wesley

24. Evening Hymn

H. Balfour Gardiner
(1877–1950)

Office hymn for Compline

From bars 43 to 54 inclusive the voices are to sing unaccompanied; the organ part is provided for rehearsal only.

91
p
A - - men A - - men A - -
A - - men A - - men A - -
- - men A - - men A - - men A - -
- - men A - - men A - - men A - -
97
- - - - - - - - - - - men.
- - - - - - - - - - - men.

25. Glorious and Powerful God
Op. 135, No. 3

Charles V. Stanford
(1852–1924)

Easter Day, 1913

26. God be in my head

Words from *Sarum Primer*

H. Walford Davies
(1869–1941)
edited by Lionel Dakers

27. God be in my head

Old English prayer

John Rutter
(b. 1945)

28. God is a spirit

from *The Woman of Samaria*

John 4: 23, 24

W. Sterndale Bennett
(1816–1875)

This anthem may either be sung accompanied or unaccompanied.

29. God so loved the world

John 3: 16, 17

John Goss
(1800–1880)

30. Haec dies

Antiphon at Vespers, etc., during
Easter week. Ps. 117: 24

Jacques Arcadelt
(b.*c.* 1510, d. 1568)
edited by John Milsom

All dynamics are editorial.

This is the day which the Lord hath made: let us rejoice and be glad therein.

31. Hide not thou thy face

Richard Farrant
(d. 1581)
edited by
Anthony Greening

Psalm 27: 10

32. Holy, Holy, Holy

Hymn to the Trinity

Reginald Heber
(1783–1826)

Peter Ilich Tchaikovsky
(1840–1893)

To the memory of Evelyn Mary Ley

33. Holy is the true light

Salisbury Diurnal by
G. H. Palmer

William H. Harris
(1883–1973)

34. If we believe

I Thessalonians 4: 14, 18

John Goss
(1800–1880)
edited by Lionel Dakers

35. If ye love me

Thomas Tallis
(c. 1505–85)
edited by
Peter le Huray

John 14: 15–17

All dynamics are editorial.

36. Jesu dulcis memoria

St. Bernard of Clairvaux
Translated by J. M. Neale

Attributed Tomás Luis de Victoria
(*c.* 1549–1611)

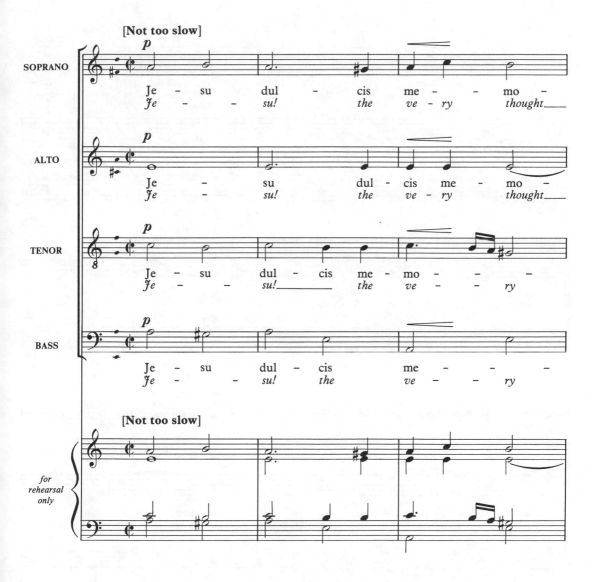

All dynamics are editorial.

37. Jesu, joy of man's desiring

from Cantata No. 147 *Herz und Mund und That und Leben*

translated by Robert Bridges
(1844–1930)

J. S. Bach
(1685–1750)
edited by H. P. Allen

1. Je - su, joy___ of
2. Through the way___ where

38. Jesu, lead my footsteps ever
from *The Christmas Oratorio, Part IV*

English translation by
C. S. Terry

J. S. Bach (1685–1750)
Arranged by Richard D. P. Jones

Je - su,_____ lead_____ my foot - steps_____
From all_____ ills_____ my do - ings_____

39. Jesu, the very thought of thee

St. Bernard
Translated by E. Caswell

Edward C. Bairstow
(1874–1946)

40. King of glory, King of peace

George Herbert
(1593–1632)

Jesu, meines Herzens Freud
J. S. Bach (1685–1750)
arranged by W. H. Harris
edited by Lionel Dakers

41. Lead me, Lord

from Praise the Lord, O my soul

Psalms 5: 8, 4: 9

Samuel Sebastian Wesley
(1810–1876)

42. Let thy merciful ears, O Lord

[? Thomas] Mudd
(b. *c.* 1560)
edited by W. S. Collins

Collect for the Tenth Sunday after Trinity

All dynamics are editorial.

43. Let us now praise famous men

R. Vaughan Williams
(1872–1958)
edited by Lionel Dakers

Ecclesiasticus 44

And some there be, which have no me - mo - ri - al; who are pe - rished, as though they had ne - ver been. Their bo - dies are bu - ried in peace; but their name liv-eth for e - ver - more.

44. Lo, round the throne a glorious band

Melody by N. Herman
arranged by Henry G. Ley
(1887–1962)
edited by Lionel Dakers

Rowland Hill
(1744–1833)

45. Locus iste

Gradual for the Dedication of a Church

Anton Bruckner
(1824–1896)

46. Lord, for thy tender mercy's sake

from J. Bull
Christian Prayers and Holy Meditations (1568)

Farrant* (16th c.)
edited by
Anthony Greening

*It is not possible to identify the composer of this anthem. Different sources describe the composer as 'John Hilton' and 'Farrant'. All dynamics are editorial.

228

47. Lord, I trust thee

from the *Brockes Passion* (1716)

Barthold Brockes
(1680–1747)
translated by
Denys Darlow

G. F. Handel
(1685–1759)
edited by
Denys Darlow

When the breath of life has left___ me,

May my soul__ be blend-ed with - - thee.

For Roy Massey, David Briggs, and Hereford Cathedral Choir

48. Mary's Magnificat

Words and music by
Andrew Carter
(b. 1939)

1. Soft - ly a light is steal - ing, Sweet - ly a maid - en sings, Ev - er wake - ful, ev - er wist - ful. Watch-ing faith - ful-ly, thank - ful-ly, tend - er-ly her

49. My eyes for beauty pine

Robert Bridges
(1844–1930)

Herbert Howells
(1892–1983)

50. My shepherd is Lord

Words from
Pilot Study on a Liturgical Psalter

Harrison Oxley
(b. 1933)

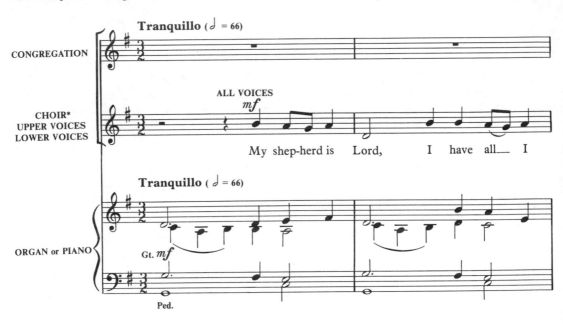

*It is not essential for the choir to divide into upper and lower voices. The setting can be sung by unison choir, lower parts and descants being omitted.

*The organ part between brackets ⌈ ⌉ is best omitted; this section is meant for voices unaccompanied.

*Alternative R.H. part for use when lower voices' part is omitted.

*For these two bars choir may sing with congregation if preferred.

51. My soul, there is a country

Henry Vaughan
(1622–1695)

C. Hubert H. Parry
(1848–1918)

52. Never weather-beaten sail

Thomas Campion
(1567–1620)

Charles Wood
(1866–1926)

53. Nolo mortem peccatoris

Thomas Morley
(1577/8–1602)
edited by
John Morehen

Text from a medieval carol

Translation: I do not wish the death of a sinner: these are the words of the Saviour.
This anthem may be sung a semitone higher. All dynamics are editorial.

written for the R.S.C.M. Canterbury Area Finals 1980

54. O come, let us sing unto the Lord

Venite, exultemus Domino

Psalm 95: 1–7

Anthony Piccolo
(b. 1953)

55. O gladsome light, O grace

translated from the Greek by
Robert Bridges
(1844–1930)

Louis Bourgeois
(c. 1510–1561)
set by Claude Goudimel
edited by Henry G. Ley

All dynamics are editorial.
This anthem may be sung unaccompanied.

Fa - ther of might un - known, Thee, His in - car - nate Son, And

Ho - ly Spi - rit a - dor - ing. 3. To thee of right be -

- longs   All   praise of ho - ly songs, O   Son of God, life - giv -

- er;   Thee, there - fore, O Most High, The   world doth glo - ri - fy,

And   shall ex - alt for ev - er. A - - - men.

56. O Holy Spirit, Lord of grace

Charles Coffin
(1676–1749)
translated by
John Chandler

Christopher Tye
c. 1505–?1572
edited by
Gerald H. Knight

All dynamics are editorial.

to F.F.

57. O how amiable

Anthem for the Dedication of a Church or other Festivals

Text from Psalms 84 and 90
and Isaac Watts (1674–1748)

R. Vaughan Williams
(1872–1958)

58. O Lord, increase our faith

Henry Loosemore
(?–1670)

All dynamics are editorial.

59. O Lord my God

King Solomon's Prayer
based on I Kings 8

S. S. Wesley
(1810–76)
edited by
H. Watkins Shaw

Wesley intended the first ending to be used when the treble part is sung by boys, and the second ending when
it is sung by women.

60. O Lord, my God, to thee

Attributed to
Jacques Arcadelt
(*c.* 1510–1568)

From Psalms 25 & 26

All dynamics are editorial.

61. O Lord, open thou our lips

Book of Common Prayer

Andrew Carter
(b. 1939)

Responses

Spoken after the creed: The Lord be with you.
Response: And with thy spirit.
Let us pray.

Our Father

62. O Lord, the maker of all things

The King's Primer 1545

William Mundy
(*c.* 1530–91)
edited by Peter le Huray

All dynamics are editorial.

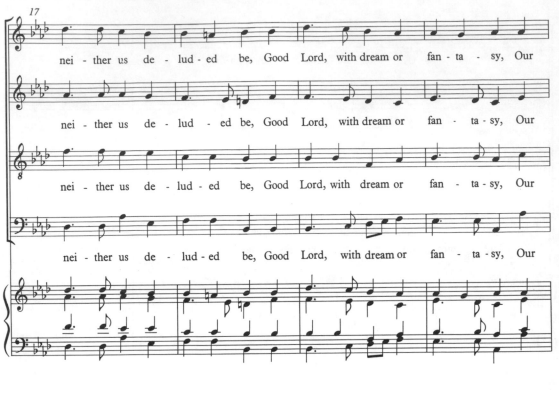

63. O Lorde, the maker of al thing

The King's Primer 1545

John Joubert
(b. 1927)

64. O quam gloriosum

English words by
C. Hylton Stewart
Antiphon at first Vespers,
Feast of All Saints

Tomás Luis de Victoria
(1548–1611)
edited by John Milsom

65. O Saviour of the world

Antiphon at the Visitation of the Sick
(Book of Common Prayer)

John Goss
(1800–1880)

This anthem may be sung without accompaniment.

66. O Saviour of the world

Antiphon at the Visitation of the Sick
(Book of Common Prayer)

Arthur Somervell
(1863–1937)

11

Sa - viour of the world, Who by thy Cross and pre - cious Blood hast re -

Sa - viour of the world, Who by thy Cross and pre - cious Blood hast re -

Sa - viour of the world, Who by thy Cross and pre - cious Blood hast re -

Sa - viour of the world, Who by thy Cross and pre - cious Blood hast re -

15

- deem - ed us, Save us and help us,

- deem - ed us, Save us and help us, we hum - bly be -

- deem - ed us, Save us and help us, and help us, we hum - bly be -

- deem - ed us, Save us and

67. O that I knew where I might find him!

Job 23: 3, 8–9
John 20: 29

W. Sterndale Bennett
(1816–1875)

This anthem should be sung unaccompanied.

58

the right hand. Bless—ed are they,— are— they that have not

%𝄋 **Arioso moderato** (♩ = 72)

the right hand. Bless—ed are they,— are— they that have not

the right hand. Bless—ed are they,— are— they that have not

the right hand. Bless — ed are they_____

%𝄋 **Arioso moderato** (♩ = 72)

64

seen, that have not seen, and yet have be-liev-ed, Bless — ed,

seen, that have not seen, and yet have be-liev-ed, Bless—ed,

seen, that have not seen, not seen, and yet have be-liev-ed, Bless — —

the that have not seen, not seen, and yet have be-liev — ed, Bless-ed,

68. O thou, the central orb

Words by
H. R. Bramley

Charles Wood
(1866–1926)

69. Oculi omnium

Gradual for the
Feast of Corpus Christi

Charles Wood
(1866–1926)

70. Panis angelicus

Camille Saint-Saëns
(1835–1921)

71. Praise, O praise

Sir H. W. Baker
(1821–1877)

Martin How
(b. 1931)

To be sung by all available voices. The optional lower parts may be sung by any Altos or Basses.

*Preferably S. A. Duet

†Any voices at written pitch, or an octave lower (for men) - or both, as convenient.

72. Praise to thee, Lord Jesus

Final Chorus of *St. Matthew Passion*

English translation by
Lucy E. Broadwood

Heinrich Schütz
(1585–1672)
edited by Richard D. P. Jones

All dynamics are editorial.

375

73. Pray that Jerusalem

C. V. Stanford (1852–1924)
edited by Lionel Dakers
Melody from
Playford's Psalms (1671)

Words from the
Scottish Psalter (1650)

sakes, Peace be in thee, I'll say.

(Sw.)   (Gt.)

And _ for the house of God _ our _ Lord, I'll seek thy

good al — — way.

74. Rejoice in the Lord alway

Henry Purcell
(*c.* 1659–1695)
arranged and edited by
Watkins Shaw

Philippians 4: 4-7

All dynamics are editorial.

75. Round me falls the night

William Romanis
(1824–1899)

Melody by Adam Drese (1620–1701)
v. 1 harm. S. S. Wesley (1810–1876)
v. 2 harm. Henry G. Ley (1887–1962)
v. 3 harm. J. S. Bach (1685–1750)

1. Round me falls the night; Saviour, be my light; Thro' the hours in darkness shrouded Let me see thy face unclouded; Let thy Glory shine In this heart of mine.

2. Earthly work is done, Earthly sounds are none; Rest in sleep and silence seeking,

76. Sacerdotes Domini

English translation by
R. R. Terry
Offertory for Corpus Christi

William Byrd
(1543–1623)
edited by John Milsom

All dynamics are editorial.

77. Salvator mundi

Giovanni Pierluigi da Palestrina
(c. 1526–94)

All dynamics are editorial.

78. Salve Regina
Op. 96 No. 5

Eleventh-century Marian Antiphon
English translation by John Vorrasi

William Mathias
(1934–1992)

Lento molto espressivo ♩ = c. 60

SOPRANO
ALTO

Sal - ve, Re - gi - na, sal - ve, Re - gi - na, Ma - ter
Hail Queen of Hea - ven, hail Queen of Hea - ven, Mo - ther

TENOR
BASS

mi - se - ri - cor - di - ae: Vi - ta, dul - ce - do,____
filled with com - pas - sion mild. Source of all sweet - ness,____

et spes____ nos - tra, sal - ve.____
and hope____ of our sal - va - tion.____

Ad te cla - ma - mus ex - su - les, fi - li - i He - vae.____
Oh hear our cry - ing, your child - ren ex - iled from E - den,____

79. Solus ad victimam

Peter Abelard
(1079–1142)
translated by
Helen Waddell

Kenneth Leighton
(1929–1988)

Let our hearts suf-fer in thy Pas - sion, Lord,__ That ve-ry suf-fer-ing

may__ thy mer - cy win.__ This is the night__ of

tears,__ the three days' space,__ Sor-row a - bi-ding of the e - ven-tide,__

Ped.

*Altos may sing an 8ve lower in this phrase if desired.

69
cresc.
ff
Hea-vy with weep-ing may the three days pass, To win the
ff
To win the
cresc.
ff
(non legato)
74
laugh - ter, the laugh - - - - ter of thine
laugh - - - ter, the laugh - - - - ter of thine
Man.
78
rit.
Eas - ter Day.
Eas - ter Day.
rit.
fff
Ped.

80. So they gave their bodies

From Pericles' Funeral Oration (Athens 431 BC)
translated by Alfred Zimmern

Peter Aston
(b. 1938)

The words are from *The Greek Commonwealth* by Alfred Zimmern (5th ed. 1931) by permission of Oxford University Press.

81. Subdue us by Thy goodness
from *Cantata No. 22*

Text translated from German of
Elisabeth Kreuziger, 1524

J. S. Bach (1685–1750)
arranged by Richard D. P. Jones
Chorale melody:
Herr Christ, der einig Gotts Sohn

All dynamics are editorial.

82. Super flumina Babylonis

Psalm 136 (137): 1

Orlande di Lassus
(c. 1532–94)

All dynamics are editorial.

83. Surgens Jesus

English text by
R. R. Terry

Peter Phillips
(1560 or 1561–1628)
edited by Lionel Pike

84. The day draws on with golden light

Aurora lucis rutilat
translated by
Thomas Alexander Lacey

Edward C. Bairstow
(1874–1946)
founded on an Angers Church Melody

The day draws on with gold - en light,

Glad songs go e - choing through the height,

The broad earth

lifts an an - swering cheer,_____ The

deep makes moan__with wail - ing fear._____

cresc.

SOPRANO and ALTO *f*

For lo,____ He comes,__ the migh - ty

TENOR and BASS Unis.

f

f

To my parents

85. The secret of Christ

Text from Isaiah 42: 14–16
Revelation 22: 1–3, and
The Pilgrim Prayer (based on Colossians 4:2-4)
by the Revd Canon Derrick Walters

Richard Shephard
(b. 1949)

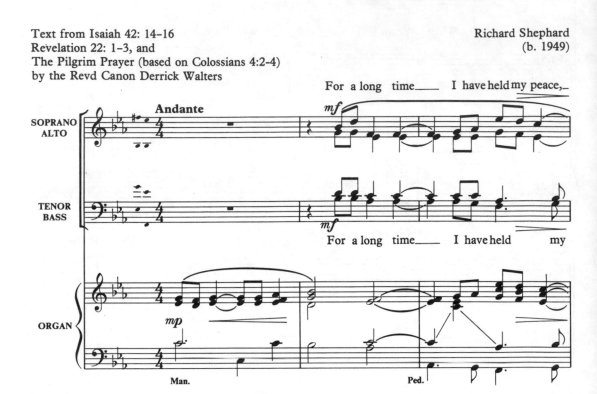

blind in a way they know____ not, in paths that they have not known I____ will guide____ them. I will turn____ their dark - ness in - to____ light, and I____ will

86. The souls of the righteous

Stanley Marchant
(1883–1949)

Wisdom 3: 1, 2

87. The strife is o'er

Henry G. Ley
(1887–1962)
Melody by Melchior Vulpius
(c. 1570–1615)
edited by Lionel Dakers

Words Anon. (18th Cent.?)
Translated by Francis Pott (1832)

Hal - le - lu - jah, Hal - le - lu - jah!

Death's migh-tiest powers have done their worst, And Je-sus hath His foes dis -

- persed; Let shouts of praise and joy out - burst: Hal - le -

*This descant is optional, and the sopranos can sing in unison with the basses if required

88. This is the record of John

Orlando Gibbons
(1583–1625)
edited by
Peter le Huray

John 1: 19

All dynamics are editorial.

unto him, What art thou? that we may give,___ that we may give an answer unto them that sent us. What sayest thou of thy-self? And he said, I am___ the voice of him that cri-eth in the wild — er-ness, Make straight the

89. Thou judge of quick and dead

from *'Let us lift up our heart'*

Bishop Wilberforce

Samuel Sebastian Wesley
(1810–1876)

90. Thou knowest, Lord

From the Burial Service

Henry Purcell
(1659–1695)

91. Thou visitest the earth

Maurice Greene
(1695–1755)

from Psalm 65

All dynamics are editorial.

484

92. Thou wilt keep him in perfect peace

Isaiah 26: 3; Psalm 139: 11;
John 1: 5; Psalm 119: 175;
The Lord's Prayer

Samuel Sebastian Wesley
(1810–1876)

93. Though I speak with the tongues of men

I Corinthians 13: 1–4, 7–9, 12–13

Edward C. Bairstow
(1874–1946)

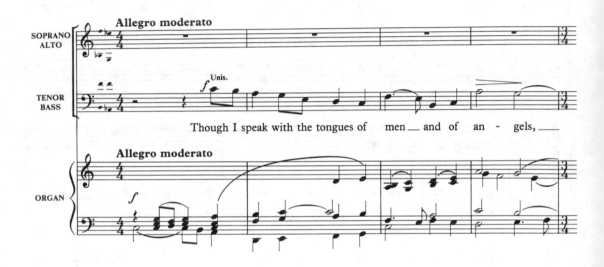

Though I speak with the tongues of men — and of an - gels, —

and have not cha - ri-ty, cha - ri-ty,

I am be - come as sound-ing

94. Turn back O Man

Melody 'the old 124th Psalm'
Arranged by Gustav Holst (1874–1934)
edited, and with organ part,
by Lionel Dakers

Clifford Bax
(1886–1962)

28

Age af-ter age their tra-gic em-pires rise. Built while they

Age af-ter age their tra-gic em-pires rise. Built while they

33

p

Earth might be fair and

dream and in that dream-ing weep.

dream and in that dream-ing weep.

73

joy man's old un-daunt-ed cry   'Earth shall be   fair, and   all her

joy man's old un-daunt-ed cry   'Earth shall be   fair, and   all her

joy man's old un-daunt-ed cry   'Earth shall be   fair, and   all her

joy man's old un-daunt-ed cry   'Earth shall be   fair, and   all her

78

folk   be   one!'

folk   be   one!'

folk   be   one!'

folk   be   one!'

95. Turn thy face from my sins

Psalm 51: 9–11

Thomas Attwood
(1765–1838)

96. Wash me throughly

Psalm 51: 2-3

Samuel Sebastian Wesley
(1810–1876)

97. When Jesus, our Lord

from *Christus (Op. 97)*

I

Matthew 2: 1-2

Felix Mendelssohn
(1809-1847)
edited by Ivor Keys

When Je-sus, our Lord, was born in Beth · le·hem, in the land of Ju · dæ · a; be·hold, from the east to the ci – ty of Je · ru · sa · lem there came the wise men and said:

II

TENOR (Solo): Say, where is he _ born, the king of Ju · dæ · a? for

BASS I (Solo): Say, where is he _ born, the king of Ju · dæ – a? for we have seen his

BASS II (Solo): Say, where _ is he _ born, the king of Ju · dæ – a? for we have

Andante

[Sempre staccato]

III
CHORUS

Numbers 24: 17
Psalm 2: 9

SOPRANO: There shall a Star from Ja - cob

ALTO: There shall a Star from Ja - cob

TENOR:

BASS:

SOPRANO: come forth, and a Scep - tre from Is - ra - el rise up,

ALTO: come forth, and a

Praise, oh praise such love o'er-flow - ing!

Praise, oh praise such love o'er-flow - ing!

Praise, oh praise such love o'er-flow - ing!

Praise, oh praise such love o'er-flow - ing!

98. When to the temple Mary went

Translated from the German by
J. Troutbeck

Johannes Eccard
(1553–1611)

All dynamics are editorial.

99. Where Thou reignest

Des Tages Weihe, D.763

Benjamin Webb
(1819–1885)
adapted by F. A. W. Docker

Franz Schubert
(1797–1828)

100. Zadok the Priest

After I Kings 1: 39–48

George Frideric Handel
(1685–1759)
edited by Lionel Dakers